Animal Acrobats

David Drew

RIGBY

Drawings by Penny Martin

Contents

Frog feet
Leopard frogs have webbed back feet that help them to push themselves out of the water.

Leopard frog

Most frogs can leap high out of the water to catch flying insects. They use their powerful back legs which are up to three times longer than their front legs.

A leopard frog can jump thirteen times its body length.

Barn swallow

A barn swallow can drink while it is flying. It can catch insects in flight as well.

Swallows can spend days in the air without coming down to land. They need to be able to feed without stopping and some travel up to 12,000 miles a year.

A swallow's bill
Swallows have a wide bill shaped like a shovel. This makes it easier for the swallow to scoop up water as it flies.

Scarab beetle

These large beetles have two wings for flying, and two wing covers that have to be held up, out of the way.

The wings beat about 20 times a second.

Flying muscles
A beetle's wings have no muscles. Instead, muscles inside its body bend its skin, and the skin moves the wings.

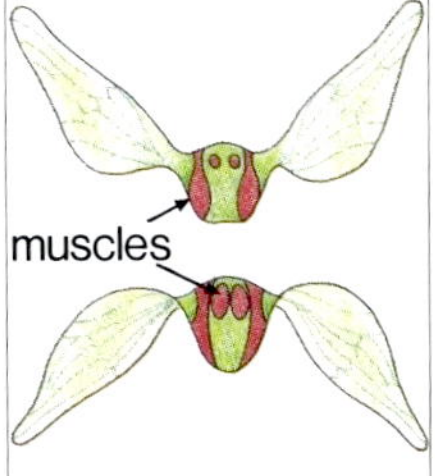

Tree frog

Some frogs climb trees and are able to glide from high branches to lower ones. They use their back feet to steer themselves.

The picture shows two images of the same frog photographed a split second apart.

Sticky toes
Tree frogs have suction pads on their toes that help them hang on to tree trunks and wet leaves.

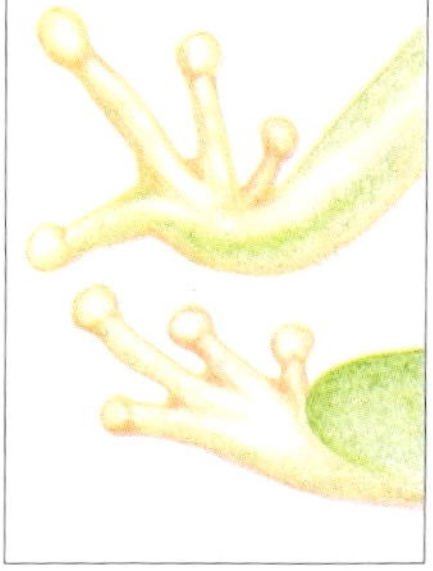

The same lacewing is shown three times in this photograph.

Lacewing

Lacewings are one of the few animals that can make a vertical take-off. They probably use this trick to escape their enemies.

A lacewing has four wings. The front and back wings on each side are moved together.

Catching lacewings
You can attract lacewings at night by putting a light near your window.
You can pick up the lacewing with a paint-brush moistened at the tip.

Sugar glider
A sugar glider has a flap of skin between its little finger and its big toe.

Sugar glider

This animal can glide from branch to branch by using the flaps of skin between its legs like a parachute. It can steer by curving the flap with its feet.

Just before it lands, the sugar glider brakes by kicking its back legs forward.

A sugar glider's body is about the size of your hand.

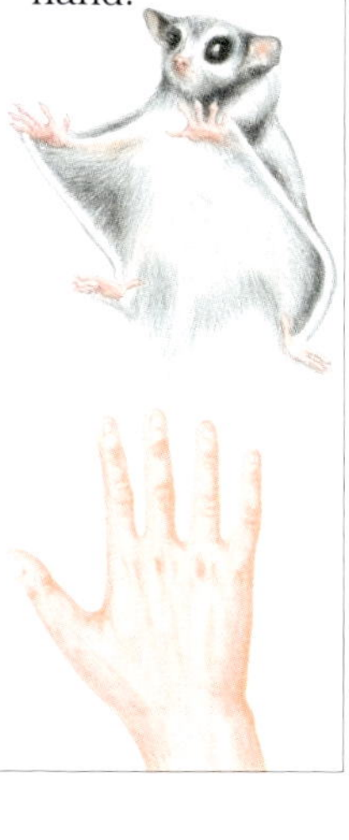

Feathertail glider
A feathertail glider has a flap of skin between its elbow and its knee.

A feathertail glider's body is smaller than your hand.

Feathertail glider

These tiny gliders can leap from tree to tree even in strong winds. They steer using their flattened tails, and they lift their tails up to slow down.

Feathertails feed at night on flowers and insects.

A kingfisher can steer its flight by bending its tail feathers.

Kingfisher

Kingfishers can dive underwater to catch their prey. They dive with their beaks open. The beak is used to catch hold of the fish, not to spear it.

The kingfisher can enter the water, catch its prey, and leave the water again in less than half a second.

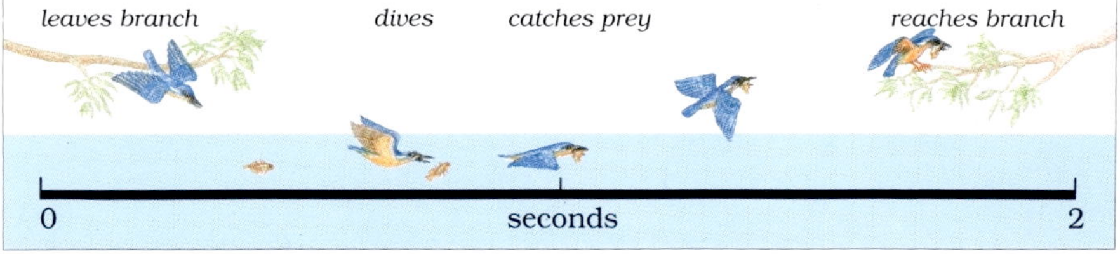

Wing size and speed
Fast birds have small, narrow wings.
Slow birds have large, broad wings.

Fast wing

Slow wing

Little owl

The wings of a bird are really its arms. The wing tip is supported by its fingers.

Birds can fly more smoothly by spreading their feathers apart. Owls are slower birds than kingfishers, but they can change direction more easily.

A kestrel, with tail feathers fanned and alula fluttering, dives on its prey.

Kestrel

A kestrel needs to be able to slow its flight as it comes in to land, to avoid crashing at high speed. It does this by fanning its tail and kicking its legs forward.

Kestrels can hover in mid-air for long periods, but only if they face into the wind.

The alula
Attached to a kestrel's wing is an extra wing, called the alula, which helps it to avoid stalling at low speeds.

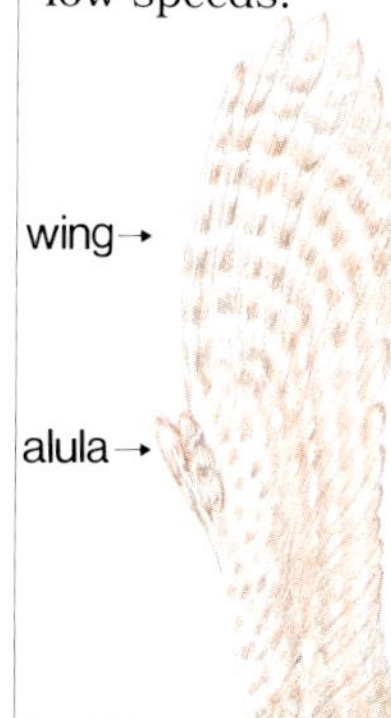

Jumping spider

This tiny jumping spider lets out a silk thread as it jumps from one rock to another. The thread acts as an anchor in case the spider slips.

A jumping spider hunts insects by leaping on top of them.

This jumping spider cannot see the fly even though it is only 2 inches away.

Archer fish usually hit their prey on the first attempt.

Archer fish

An archer fish can "shoot" insects with a squirt of water. When the insect is wet it cannot fly, so it tumbles into the water and the fish swallows it.

An archer fish can "shoot" at its prey up to 3 feet away.

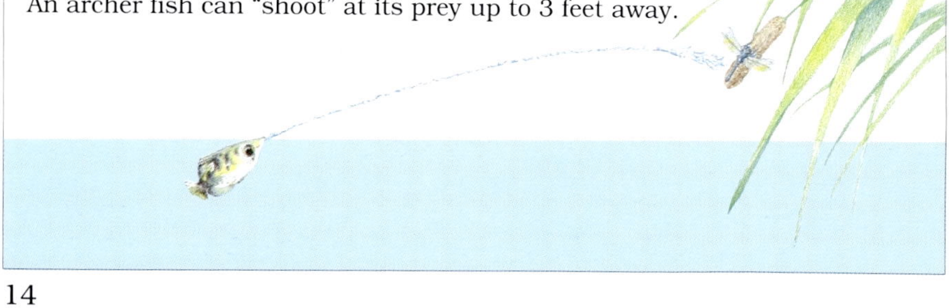

Chameleon

A chameleon catches its prey by unrolling its sticky tongue. Some chameleons can catch birds with their tongues. When the chameleon pokes its tongue out, it has to hold on to a branch with its tail, or it would fall over.

A chameleon's tongue is as long as its body.

A mouse-eared bat approaches a cricket on top of a tree stump. Bats can find their way in the dark by sending out high-pitched sounds and listening for the echoes that bounce off the objects around them.

Bat

A bat's wings are giant hands. The bones inside its wings are its fingers. The claw that sticks out is its thumb.

Some bats can catch fish while flying over a stream by dragging the claws of their back feet along the water.

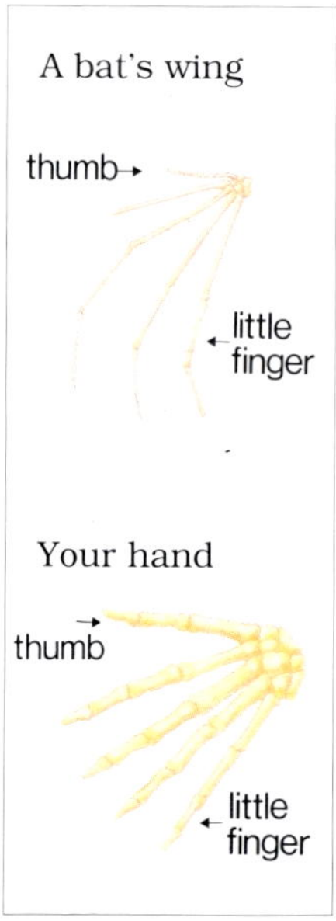